BECOMING RIBBONS

BECOMING RIBBONS

Poems   Amber Adams

First printing

ISBN 978-0-87775-092-5 (paperback)
ISBN 978-0-87775-094-9 (cloth)

COVER. "Lockdown 249" by Tania Chanter." Photograph courtesy of the artist.

∞
This book is printed on Mohawk Via, which is acid-free and meets ANSI standards for archival permanence.

Printed in the United States of America

Unicorn Press
Post Office Box 5523
Greensboro, NC 27435

www.unicorn-press.org

For Brad

Killed, we say, if a war zone. Kept, we say,
if a woman. Love-love we say when the score is
zero. Irrelevant, says the sea into which
everything we throw away ends up, words.

LISA OLSTEIN, "Built For It"

BECOMING RIBBONS

BECOMING RIBBONS

KLEOS

The banded ribbons
of color on your Marine uniform
and the beginning curl when your hair
grew out—details dulling like brass.
I can no longer trust memory
oxidized by hours. Living
changes the past in unnoticeable ways.

I keep a ritual of small artifacts: razor
clamshell, dogs tags, keyhole limpets, a Marine
Corps button with thread hung loose, letters
in blue ink. Spread out before me they plot
a small cemetery.

When I am in the flood of regret, I try to connect
each remnant to the outcome: each shell
to its former inhabitant, like an explanation.

There was a time before you were emptied,
before you were shaped by the lockstep
of orders. Consider the years desensitized.
Consider the silhouettes peppered with practice bullets,

each backlit figure galvanized to details:
This one sways with his daughter
in his arms; this one removes his flak vest
and lays down his rifle to swim
in the Euphrates River; this one holds
his shoes and walks along the moonlit beach.

Their dark targets survived in you,
each a shadow-life marked out of existence.

he embarked

to become

In September, 2002, *enlisted*

Following his recruit training, he was assigned

Private First Class

Marines

gained the ranks of

three combat deployments to

Iraq

THE WEIGHT OF A BIRD

We drove your blue Mustang across state lines
                                so fast we spun out
promises on highway lines and vandalized
time as if it were an exit sign. I found a ring
                        on your dog tags
and we were halfway to San Francisco
before the thought: we might
                                beat the guilt

or the rain. In Fisherman's Wharf we cracked open
                crab legs over tell-alls, and I changed my mind

about Pinot Grigio, the lemon and sweet apple
blossomed a summer
                        in November.

*

You asked if I wanted
to meet your great-grandparents, and we took the BART
to Oakland. You went hunting
                        with your great-grandfather.
Your great-grandmother (was she part Strega?) incanted:
                                to pluck
a bird was to make a man
                        happy. When you came

back I was wrist deep in pheasant down,
                              pulling calamus from skin.

*

I need you to know: I was so ready
to be your wife.
                    I would have delivered

my stippled body on silver to prove I was
unsure and just
                    cruel enough for marriage.

ARMY SERVICE RIBBON

The day before I left for basic training,
I discovered that I was capable of holding
myself hostage, muzzle to the rib
of intuition. Sleepless, I called you
from the hotel, *My life—I am not meant for this.*

Then you were kissing
the ocean from my face. You knew—
"Don't listen to anyone
else but me; you can do this."

And I learned how to sleep
while pushing my body up from the floor,
learned how to hide my lettered thoughts
under a thin blanket, learned how
to chamber a round and speak a language
made of rifled syllables and camouflaged
aggression. I became moss oak and shadow
and crawled under a live arc
of tracer bullets, like shooting
stars across the South Carolina sky.

I never asked myself the why of it,
just if I could. At night, shining
my boots, I smudged out reflection.

CALLING YOU FROM FT. JACKSON

I held the hard coil of the pay phone line
as you told me

of the car wreck—your ex
beside you,

the seatbelt secrets that flew through
the windshield

like a second DUI. There was nothing
worth the platitude of saying,

nothing except the nothing which
wasn't bearable,

I'm Sorry I'm sorry i'm sorry.
A dare:

Leave me. I don't want to feel.

We were already prisoners
of war,

tapping at the walls, trying
to get through.

Did you hear me? Your shame was doggish
and bittersweet.

I, too,
was reckless with things

I loved.
I could have granted you clemency

like no court,
but I was afraid

you wanted
to see what an ending truly was.

SOLEMNLY SPOKEN

Older still, this story moves through us like spilled
wedding wine incises white pleats of organza
silk smooth as vows voiced—in the blaze

of invasion you must commit or lose everything.
At nineteen, vows will break you to make,
I take you and *I do solemnly swear that I will
support and defend the Constitution of the United States
against all enemies, foreign and domestic* and surely
goodness and mercy all of the days of my life.
                              [So help me God]

Bear this and make allegiance to the same, for I do not want,
except this small piece of land, building
with skin and clavicle, scapula and nails,
pale legs enfolded in tan, as olive wood
bedposts—and I will dwell in this house forever.
                              [So help me God]

GLENWOOD SPRINGS

In those vapor caves, we blossomed like saxifrage
breaking expanses. Sweat rising to pore, we felt
the earth deep then, salt and sulfur-locked geological
epochs—days from our vows fortified in the confluence of rivers.

Years after, when your memorial unearthed limestone,
words cracked from their meaning. There was no
place for wildflower buds or the greenness we were. Only
your name, coming from the first man—coming from the Hebrew
earth—resounds at the end of my name. Oaths mouthed on the ears
of past lovers aren't written in funeral pamphlets.

UNFORTIFIED

Your body, away at war with
itself—fighting its very sleep.
At night, your tattoos lifted
from your skin, spotlighting
St. Michael, plucking the feather
from your leg and wielding it as a sword,
fighting the lion from your scapula.

The Marine Corps bulldog,
from over your heart, its wide
drill sergeant hat barking
Blood makes the grass grow green,
and the flag unfurling

with the uprising in your chest.
In our dreams, our children would run
disaster with grass-stained feet, protected
by the barbed wire of your bicep,
sharp at the boundary of consciousness.

BEFORE LEAVING

That morning at Hanging Lake—pulled from dark reasoning
to awakeness by the shivers of the trees and shifts
of our tent, the aspen leaves changing to orange-yellow
as their roots crawled through acres of mountains
interweaving underneath, the reach of needful hands.
How do moments exist past their making?
In the sketch of sight we felt our lives ripple out—
explosions happening on two-week leaves
grown from the spent casings of this war,
with gunmetal knowledge replacing language with
field manuals and empty acronyms
of OIF blurring into OEF and the cyclone
of war constantly enduring while losing
distinction in one great fog around us.
I lay my head down—on the pillow
of your handgun, safe and at the ready.

FRAGMENTATION

In letters from you, words were pomegranate
seeds on the desert sand fallen from husk,
cracked open. Heat-split, the door reverberating—
shaking the skeleton dust of Fallujah.
You wrote and you wrote because language
clicks in a grenade fist, grenade with the pulp
of heart, grenades as they were tattooed to your ribs
in haste the month before deployment, an unrelenting
armament of grooved iron on tender flesh. Pin pulled,
a prophecy erupts from a tattoo gun.

Looking for your face I awake in the drive down
State Route 1, the coastal curves and pickup truck
bench seat, my head in your lap hours before your battalion
loaded buses for deployment when there was nobody but you
among the sea of Marines with your M4 and duffel bags.
Before the ground wave's impact: change before felt
before heard, boot hitting door—your face before leaving.

THE CROSSING

In those dark hours of silence your letters unfolded
the gentle current of Haditha Dam removed of the weight of your military
uniform—flak vest kevlar insignia—the elemental movements of your high
school body extended *slow is smooth smooth is quick* you cut through the surface
impelling yourself buoyant and unresisting the water holding you as before
the undertow of this war when your records at the neighborhood pool made you proud
I think of how the cadence of these motions eased into your body there
in the Euphrates River before your mind recalled the smell of chlorine and sunscreen
Saturday morning swim meets the triumph of those moments when memory
surged and the movements seemed to rise out of you borne from the great cry
of the crowd there in the river between these two worlds where one folds into the other
through each stroke reminding you of the effortlessness you had always
known in water your wedding ring slipped off your hand to the murk
drawn by the venerable force that takes that which is in motion the underworld reached
out for your hand in her hand and found payment which bound you to the passage

CENOTAPH

After his second deployment, he stacked beer cans into towering windowsill monuments. Maddening the mind's urge to build when one has seen ruins. Baghdad withstood the assault. But language? Which is to say the people, invaded and invader, bore the vicissitudes. What is conviction but the muezzin's continual call for almightiness, amidst a mortar's reach? This might be all there is left. At home in those sentinel hours, his vigil for living annihilation, light slipped around empty cans—awakening him from the dream of being home.

ENDURING FREEDOM

I received my deployment orders, an impossibility
with all we had survived. You had known the desert's fire
and survived it twice, but I was a soldier of happenstance—
caught in enlistment's wide net. We questioned
whether to have a child, to change the sentence. A nautilus
unfolding within me, cirri shaping into such detailed
softness. I imagined a small pink heart arising
from the darkest sea. It's uninteresting to think
of what could have been different if we hadn't chosen
war together—if we hadn't the violence of the ocean
lapping between us.

In the mornings, I feel the pain of another
life, its smaller victories and forfeits—of a family
fighting for time, quiet moments at dawn, before
the explosive awakening and growing of children
wanting—the holystone of laundry and dishes.
What does it matter that we trade one battle
for another? As we grow, we seal off the camerae
we can no longer live in, moving around the curvature
of ourselves, becoming something other.

FOR YOU, CHILD, WHO NEVER CAME

You must know we believed
        we had time, that the future was something
          we were capable of

suspending. You, whom I will never know, waiting
        in the caldera of Olympus Mons with the not-yet others,
          even still

you were the best possibility. The wind howls
        your absence like a dry storm.

DEPLOYMENT

They tell you of the sun wave and moon dust,
but not the loneliness—counting
days, fending off thoughts of home.
They do not tell you how much you forget,
a kind forgetting, so you can skip like a stone over

the surface of the earth through Toronto,
Shannon, Heidelberg, Turkey, and Kuwait,
each place blurring into one sleepless night.

Your letters stopped coming
before I left the States. Anything that could not
hold in the salt-heat shamal of the desert devolved
                                    [the girl I was]

to the flat-bellied lizard
of the landscape, muted brown and gray, shedding
the skins of previous selves in spined exoskeletons.

There was no return—only survival.
I did not let go of your dog tag, your metallic
last letter. I left the desert, which means to leave itself.

BAPTISM—CAMP ARIFJAN, KUWAIT

I walked into turquoise pool water
gym shorts ballooning
cotton Army t-shirt pulled around my body
feet unsettling sand on the vermiculite bottom
light rippling through chlorination

as the Army chaplain guided me back and the cold poured
through the thick of my hair down to my scalp
I should have thought of God

and yet the memories came like rising bubbles
the inhale of synthetic nylon and swim-cap rubber
from the Speedo shop where your mother worked

the mineral springs heat around my legs
enclosing your body the sudden exhale of breath
then water the water that pulled us away

from the California coast the time we chased
the tide and lost when my body was a place of worship
singing ocean hymns the Pacific waves knocking us

back fully clothed to a time free of direct orders and COs
the unholiness of plastic chairs in the on-post
chapel looking for faith in the months that piled up
when no water felt like prayer.

COMING HOME

When they say, "But you enlisted.
You signed up for this," let the anthem
of their teenage beliefs ricochet like bullets.

Let the laugh of college or open-office
chatter deafen like a C-130. Let their bodies
ache from missing their lover's thumb across
their lips. Let them beg for suburban green grass
underfoot, to supplicate the cypress knees
of Louisiana swamps. Let the sandstone
spires in Arizona tribal lands become
a holy pilgrimage.

Let them stand in an airport hangar after a year
overseas and watch families shift uncomfortably
with military pomp, squinting for recognition
in a battalion of camouflage. Let them stand there,
as I did, with no welcome.

Iraq
immediately redeployed

Iraq

Corporal to
Sergeant *executed over*
which resulted in

redeployed to Iraq

served as

personal security
serving in

I.E.D. attack
significant injuries.

OPERATION PEGASUS BRIDGE

Walking point in Al-Anbar province,
Cpl. Stokes attempted to clear the road
of buried lightning and munitions.

Once, he'd said, "My medal was just living,"
and in an instant he wasn't.

His name, you said his name,
the resonance of him traveling the air.
Staggering, you made your way between
land mines to his body and found
yourself holding him

as he died. The helicopter came,
shaking dust into the sky. Rotor blades
beat like great wings
and when the metal touched down

you gave way to injury, a wellspring
of his blood, your blood, soaked through camouflage.

You wouldn't remember the flight
but never forgot the thunder.

OCEANSIDE

Concertina wire strangles empty bases,
from the Halls of Montezuma,
to the shores of Tripoli.
Put your ear to the ground
and hear those anti-tank mines hum.

Once, we raised glasses to eagle,
globe, and anchor on the beaches
of Camp Pendleton, ran into the sea
and washed up as sunrise kelp.

We fight our country's battles
in the air, on land, and sea,

between sheets and toward each other—and find
the sea doesn't always return the same man.
Waters divide us. Here in our time,
of this we must tell, before the ocean
returns to cover our mouths.

CORPORAL STOKES

The convoy: antiphonal scream to the minarets'
prayer call. A landscape teetering with assault.
Everyone who fights thinks they are beaten
and strong at the same time. An explosion changes
everything, a reversal of time.

Blast returns to mold, returns to click,
returns to scrap metal fragments held,
and the four of us on a backyard patio
with Blue Moons and the softening of twice-baked
potatoes in charred foil. In the sun-bleached
blue of his eyes I say, *take care of my husband over there.*

Out of that moment, inexplicable echoes. Heat flux
the sudden flame, corporal, corporeal—of the body
of troops, a posthumous silver star.

POLEMOLOGY

It began with confusion, with the other
and weapons; with rock, gun, improvised
explosives, biological and nuclear. Taking another
out of the equation, the subtraction and division
of how to survive. The war in Iraq
began between Sumer and Elam.

History is a match of capture
the flag, making prisoners or winners
of those that cross imaginary
lines. It's a matter of endurance, *amor
patriae*, of love. In the way of fathers

a birthright. A person, a product,
meaning of this land, laying opposite
or spread before one, a country
fresh, as in fresh air, open to take,
as in free.

MEDEVAC

Open,
daisy chains blossom when a pressure plate trip
travels the wire. A surface violence,
           an excess of light.
Each body torn open diagrams a metal pathway.
All tissue is soft and taken away in flights.
He dies, you live. In Bethesda
morphine cannot stop his body becoming
           ribbons.

THE FOX AND THE LION

The first deployment, the fox went running.
The lion prowled for a fight, up-armored,
leaving a trail of links and brass. The lion
strolled through the streets of Fallujah
watching buildings fall as if fate-named.

The second deployment, the fox became sly.
Dancing about as the lion searched
for weapon caches. The fox realizing:
this is a game.

By the third deployment the fox planted
remote-controlled explosives, and watched
as the sun-baked lion slunk forward to discover
light in the sizzle of shrapnel.

I want to hold the thick sling of your jaw,
stroke back your golden fur and remind you,
you were never meant to hunt fox.

WALTER REED HOSPITAL

Sometime after the transports, the ambulance's
primal cry, the rush fever of Bethesda, after
surgery, war teeth extracted from your side,
the swarm of hands and fervor, after
the stitches, burn grafts, transfusions—after
the phone call clouded with opiates. You said,
I don't want you to see me like this.

Sometime beginning with the presidential
handshake, and the smallness of your body
after weeks without movement,

sometime then, I realized
you weren't coming back.

SEMPER FIDELIS

And yet he returned with tender skin pink
where the fragments of metal dug into the sinews
like roots in the arms I spent months waiting
to feel. The explosion ignited my name out
of him, and the words grew *I want to go back*
and kill those haji fuckers

        He dreams

his friend back into the world, and each night
earth erupts with smoke and silence in an endless
desert haze, sieges of phantoms under skin—the familiar
touch of a rifle-infiltrated night. When the fog
clears he says, *'Til now I'd hoped*

                that I alone would die.

§ 3

served as   the Nation

        focused on   recovery   from
injuries

        medically retired from the Marine Corps

                        returned to
civilian

        Site Exploitation
was responsible for   all aspects of
Intermediate Search/
                    Asymmetric Threat   Tactical
Analysis   Tactical Questioning and
                    in both

IMPROVISED EXPLOSIVE DEVICE

From Karmah, Iraq   to a coffee shop in Denver
       the quick collision of worlds, and before me
flesh of stitches,   burn dimples,   rerouted
viscera, the valved   voice of the body
       betraying itself,   a hidden colostomy bag.
We do not choose   our lives,   they choose
       us. It is in the very bones   of naming

akhos meaning "pain, grief"   and *laos* "the people"

—Achilles. Pantheons   we reenact as if

possessed. I arrive,   as if arriving

       had not always meant the end, but perhaps

an entreaty   not to be afraid. We think

of the body as separate fixtures,   destruction

localized   and repaired.   The terror

       of insurgency is always possible

          by loving someone.   You talk of the city's

open   landscape,   the unruly weapons trade,

         and we s i d e s t e p buried landmines.

UPON GETTING A JOB AFTER DEPLOYMENT

There will be a woman at a coffee shop
who will begrudge your need for hot coffee
until the day you show up in uniform,
then she will thank you for your service.
The next day, you will be both women.
At once, you will be overexperienced
and underqualified, and you will not be trusted
to make a latte, but you will have expert marks
with a grenade launcher. There will be confusion.
Do you have PTSD? Will you go postal?
Fling milk jugs at visions of insurgents?
What they mean to ask is: are you dangerous?

Customers have been looking for you,
as they think we should just bomb the hell
out of this whole idea of a normal conversation.
They would like you to know that they support
the troops, penciling in their eleven-cent tip.

LEAVING YOU

It was simply an archive erased—
a palimpsest scraped off with a razor.

DIVORCE PAPERS

As we act, let us not become the evil that we deplore.
BARBARA LEE

You said anger would come back just like the love did
just as the waves

And I felt it then—*authorized to use*

all necessary and appropriate force.

There was no line

[I divorced you because]

no word or addendum

in order to prevent any future

acts of international terrorism

again   against

U   S

WHEN I PAWNED THE RING

the jeweler said there was a flaw
in the diamond so big

that you could see it
with the naked eye. I looked

for a dark cloud along
the facet's edge. I hadn't seen

it before, and still couldn't.
Under the loupe

a small Andromeda
appeared, its sorrow-milk

spin caught in mid-turn.
I imagined that if you zoomed

in, you could see spindrift & seagulls
circling the great rock

where I stood. The guy offered
me $300. I asked if he would

throw in the pair of teardrop
pearl earrings. There was something

dramatic and true in their opalescent
sadness—the oysters

in their rumination, brine tumbling
that which refuses to leave.

What are pearls
but thoughts in the making?

Walking out of the shop I almost—
no, did convince myself—

the diamond would be loved again.

MISSING

I imagine pieces of
you scattered star grains
of sand covered in blood
blown over the landscape
of Iraq until they are no
longer distinguishable as
if you never lost the
best of you to Karmah
which fell to the hands
of ISIS in 2014 war
and memory grows over
like grapevines plump
with leaves trying to find
root in California or any
place big enough for the
ecstasy of catastrophe that rattled
within as you drove down the
coast on your Softail Harley-
Davidson a once-shared desire to
escape to remote eons miles rushing
past to remote futures that burn
out like the sun or go down
like icebergs into the
water from which
we all came.

NO ONE LEFT BEHIND

Around his wrist, the black memorial bracelet catches
light in grooves of silver. Atrophic scars scatter up
his arm where his body cannot forget his dying friend.

She stands before the man who held
her fiancé as he died. Her fingers run over
trenched skin feeling through him her lover's
goodbye. She needs to forget,
to remember, to be someone else

to touch him again. The phantasm
of her own body, its edges. She traces
the current of grief along
his body and finds her own. Both lost.
He, a friend. She, a lover.

Recursive, replicant, they see their pain
                    in each other
like mirrors that should have been covered.

BACK AZIMUTH IS THIS

Echo of a bird's sound thrums the night.
Cartographic the way a clock can bring back,
draft the room of memory, sketch the bed and dresser—
the safe for your rifles. Each a landmark returning
the shape of it, a spatial relation magnetic as the North's pull.
The night you told me you married again,
your voice already receded into the waves
of the Pacific, I could not shut out the sound,
could not see that remapping where we had been.
The tenderness of thought's reconnaissance
kept me from seeing your face but I imagined acres
of grapevines, the parallax of the sun pulling them to fruit.
Mountains to your past, and before you
birds calling as a woman hangs a star-shaped feeder.

ESPRIT DE CORPS

1

I have visions of your life there
in the unfocus of imagination. Seeing you
on a beach in the freshness of fatherhood—
wading through the coastal water holding
your daughter's miraculous hands.

2

The gulls that circle like ghosts,
the ache of living, foam-shot with loss.
The way the ocean never ceases to pull back
to itself, even as it reaches for the shore.

3

You once said suicide was the fool's way:
a war we all make with our own choices.
How simply we thought then
when terror was outside ourselves.

4

All the different waves broke the surf
that night: *husband, indifference, desire,
death.* The gull in you rose up
like a soul. I loved you most
when I was relieved of doing so.

PHOTOSYNTHESIS

after Mark Tredinnick

War has flooded the tributaries of her heart, and she beats violence.
There are boxes
of her life; the preserved wedding dress in her parents' basement marooned

with the rest, beneath the window well that fills each year, and spills rot
water over, rises
the netted happiness of tulle. She is a levee, break.

Is it possible, she asks, to despair like water? Evaporate in reaching
for the sun?
She feels like she has become nothing of what she was.

Firepower, he thinks, is schizophrenic and hallucinating itself. Believing
its fairness, he talks to himself
a world of righteousness and fresh flex, smelling gun oil

on his fingertips. Lucid a moment, quick, he sees the potential for ruin,
fears his own body
and trembles until the destruction passes. For weeks he ignites mania.

War is the savage panic possessing us all. Occasionally incoherent with it,
she torrents through her belief
of love and engulfs everything. When the storms settle, if they settle,

they will breathe a new silence, in which the inhale will be grief,
and the exhale will bloom

poppies, and she will walk through the fields of red, finding at last, her start.

PERMANENT WINTER

Snow made the world white—without secrets,

I tried to unimagine it, hundreds of times—the fight

on your lips, the bullet charged by your own hand.

You said once, you can only tell friends and family so much—

thoughts folded in letters I have read thin

as the division between this world   and the next

no true division   as if we ended there.

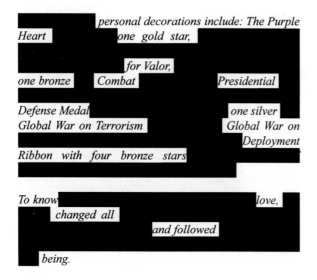

personal decorations include: The Purple
Heart   *one gold star,*

                for Valor,
one bronze   *Combat*   *Presidential*

Defense Medal   *one silver*
Global War on Terrorism   *Global War on*
                                Deployment
Ribbon with four bronze stars

To know   *love,*
    changed all
                and followed

    being.

WHERE WE STARTED

We woke to the clothes-scattered floor
            and the promises of the previous night dry in our mouths.
Last of the questions asked, except one. The morning squirmed
with formalities, and I stood at the edge of responsibility,
made my way late to class with the distraction of your touch impressed
on my naked mind.

        It takes the breath out of learning.

I say to myself:
you lose enough, and you find yourself taking with abandon. Like the drowning
or the damned, you allow yourself the desire to live. I came home
to find you strumming my guitar. There was no metaphor—

THE LION AND THE MOUSE

Durkheim states: *But everything is readily explained*
when it is recognized that the profession of a soldier
develops a moral constitution powerfully
predisposing man to make away with himself.

Once there was a lion who spared a mouse.
Later when the lion was netted by hunters, the mouse
chewed and chewed through the ropes but was unable to free
the lion despite the lion's prior mercy. We can't always
save one another, but we can commit ourselves in the making
of another's presence

for this constitution naturally occurs, in varying degrees,
among most of those who live or who have lived under the colors,
and as this is an eminently favorable soil for suicides

prowling under contractual obligation, heart-hungry
we had talked of some future time when things would slow,
and our lives would no longer be dictated by the mandates of deployments.
A time that spread out like savanna. Had you felt it then—

little is needed to actualize the tendency to self-destruction
which it contains; an example is enough. So it spreads like a trail
of gunpowder among persons thus prepared to follow it

to the very end of belief, the net of war's unmaking.
Nine days after your death the final
troops prepared to leave Iraq.

LIMINAL

Over a thousand miles away,
I slept in my childhood bedroom, bruise-
cheeked from a wisdom tooth extraction

still tingling of painkillers. Morpheus,
the god of dreams, arrived on a white boat
and I swam the river of oblivion

unaware of the chambered round
or the explosion tearing through twenty-eight years
like the rip of paper. Unaware of the police

reports or the bureaucracy of dying
trying to summarize or codify meaning.
Facts that continued to collect

up to and after your memorial. Such as:
your ashes weighed eight pounds.
Everyone surprised at the amount.

Your ashes weighed eight pounds,
same as when you came into this world.
Beginning and ending with the weight of infinity.

SHELLS

I opened the jar of shells
and pieces of glass beachcombed
that last summer when the ocean gave
and gave way to a time before the echo
of the shell was my own voice-thought.

I miss that iridescence of sound,
that component breath trembling, cavernous
as an organ, in the hallows of atrium and ventricle,
guarded chambers cracked open.

Something lived here once. Before the strike
of a firing pin emptied the weight of it. A cartridge
made perfect blank with unsaid.

BEFORE YOUR MEMORIAL

the lying began. At the bar, your friends
talked of how you left for boot camp
with a sack of apples, needing nothing other
than the orchard of your own sweat.

How you were a hero. Maybe that one
is true, if you believe a Purple Heart
has the face of George Washington.

They all wanted to be so close
to you then. If they actually knew—
loving you was like the swing

of an axe—unwieldy   but the arc!
A force split to the very core. Then
they might know how we fed the fire.

OPERATION PHANTOM FURY

My photographs, used to shape another life,
                              a violence I couldn't anticipate—

the erasure of me in how we made each other. Your widow
                              refused sympathies or
                                        poems.
                                                  She could not see my
                                                            suffering has a voice.

Suffering has a voice
              she could not see. My
                    poems
                          refused sympathies or
                                the erasure of me in how we made each other. Your widow,
                    a violence I couldn't anticipate.

My photographs used to shape another life.

YOUR MEMORIAL

I thought of the scar raised from your skin
when you lost your tattoo in the wild flame
of war lightning. The image of St. Michael's
high strike hued with burn, swirled in peach,
thick petal roses blooming from skin. Healing
culled the angel and left a flush of perennial blossoms

open and opening. At your memorial, flowers
praised their reclamation. Orchid jaws gaped
in eulogy. Gladioli sang hymns. A processional
of chrysanthemums reached out. Mockingly,
hyacinths curled like the shrapnel that never left you.
When they listed your awards I thought:

for a moment   only
                   you came back.

ELEGY FOR MODAL AUXILIARIES

            [should have]

spoken

            [could have]

prevented the end

            [would have]

taken the gun

            [should have]

buried it

            [might have]

been a seed

            [would have]

never grown

            [should have]

tried

            [would have]

been too late

AFTER YOUR MEMORIAL

You weren't even there, at the service. Only
photographs and flowers. Your body already
atomized into ash and air for the other memorial in California.

I had not expected my body to remain quiet
as memories had gone to the fire
with you the week before. I had not expected to survive

whole years disintegrating off me or the insistence
of the world pushing forward while I reached back
toward you.

I had been afraid that I would no longer be brave.
That thing I took from you and never returned
like a sweater or a name, I believed it would fall

away and I would stand before your mother
with an apology so close to my lips that I would
collapse, but instead I found myself kneeling

next to your aunt telling her about my graduate
program, making up stories about my success
because there is no place like a church

to begin believing in yourself.

CLIFF DIVING

You, leaping from the limestone bluffs of Pueblo Reservoir,
                are suspended a moment
                      with the pelicans, white K-Swiss laces fluttering, red life vest

bright as Mars in the elated air. This moment, yours as much as mine,
                collides with the surface. Memory,
             it seems, is inseparable as water,

indistinguishable. Always there and yet never
             the same, always
            the slipping glint of a fish tail reflecting the sun.

Your wife believes that she took you, an urn of your ash,
             to California. Yet,
            here you are, bobbing up from the bluegill depths

laughing the lake shale loose.

THE COST OF FLIGHT

Seven years ago,
in a house I rented briefly,
where a deadbolt door led to my bedroom
from outside, I could hear morning
by the meadowlarks' melody. Those love-starved
attention seekers never showed themselves.
Just called out, like old relationships
in the soft hue of thought.

He used to say, "One day, baby, one day,"
and on some road of hope
the calendar days marked off
like exit ramps with weeds grown over.
It's true, it turns out, that birds make
nests from tumbleweeds.

How many homes must I vacate
to learn that "one day"
was not, as it seemed, a place to settle down,
spend weekends flipping pancakes—
that for us, it was the air currents
that pulled us onward?

Suppose we stayed married after
the war. Suppose that when I hear
birds, I mean the the whip blade
rotors of helicopters. Suppose
he never died. Suppose so many
never died. The thoughts go round
and round.

When I revolve back to it
in my mind, I think of the hollowness
of bird bones. Empty little cathedrals,
where I could light candle after candle
and hide out in the rafters watching
the wax unfold into nothing.

Can a person gift themselves a future
when she no longer feels it
in her bones? What I thought
was the direction of contradiction
was actually a perfect arc.

I lived in many places, a great northern
migration. I started to question
whether I had an aerial view
of my self-dissolution. Everywhere
I looked I saw feathers.

I struggled to find my things each time
I landed. I would unpack boxes
and months later, be disappointed
by small absences.

The tragedy of birds is their emptiness:
the way every part of them is designed
for flight. Aerodynamic, they never feel
the weight of always leaving.

THE BATTLE OF THE ECLIPSE

There is no suicide in our time / unrelated to history
DENISE LEVERTOV

Just imagine: light fading from spears
and desert pinnacles, Lydian and Median warriors
looking to the sky to see their downfall foretold.

Currents of shadow bands fanned
the battlefield as the moon bit through
the sun, a sudden disappearance of day. The war stopped

as three celestial bodies, an ellipsis,
came into perfect alignment. I dream
of all wars that didn't lead to your suicide.

What does it take? What doesn't it take?
There in the sky, your unfinished
life hangs in the cerement clouds.

I keep coming back to it: the way your mind
turned on itself—became war itself—after endless,
elliptical rotations

between here and Iraq. Inevitable
deployments, inevitable danger, inevitable
heat, inedible MREs, incomings,

invasion of phosphorus dreams, insomniac. A fugue
state let slip your own birthright, a boy
looking up at the sky with a pinhole

camera made of cardboard and aluminum foil. Awe
is something so easy to create that we forget.
Any eclipse is worth stopping for . . .

any suicide is an eclipse.

FAST STAR

Here I am in this future
and it is nothing like we talked about,
in that time when we were young.

Except that I still over-express
myself in these little letters to you.
That is the same.

Express meaning both
fast and to tell one's feeling.
You were express expression,

which is why so many women
believed you, and why I always
knew you would be a fast star,

a blaze in the atmosphere
of my twenties. What I didn't know
was the part just after,

how I would remember the bright of you,
(the luck of it!) long after you went dark.

HOLLOWNESS MAKES A CRESTING WAVE

I found myself on the dance floor
at a wedding, years after I became

someone else. Your father was there—
a stone breaking the surface of the continual

present. Once I was his daughter-in-law.
The fact shocks me with intimacy,

an indivisible relation that enters
like a ghost through a wall. Suddenly

we were dancing, father and daughter.
A backward look, green dress trailing

in an upswell of music. This does not mean
nothing. Rising up like the tide, we remembered

you who brought us together
when I was a girl who disappeared

and returned a woman, without you.

A LAND MORE KIND

> To lose the earth you know, for greater knowing; to lose
> the life you have, for greater life; to leave the friends you
> loved, for greater loving; to find a land more kind than
> home, more large than earth—
> THOMAS WOLFE

Today I think of marriage,
the man before me a wellspring
of hours we have yet to live—our children,
the laundry in unfolded haystacks, the comb and tangle
of hair on wind-whipped evenings. We will always
be fighting the unruly, something ready
to overtake us. And marriage? Who
are we to believe in something?

I have been here before, once,
vows made on a dandelion seed head
scattered in the hot air of the world.

From my first marriage, I fashioned
a stone boat and loaded it with marble.
I did not want to forget that the earth could
make something that lasts.

With it I made poems, headstone lines—
and they are—etched with sorrowful chisels.
It pains me to have loved. To feel carved out,
to be filled again.

Is this faithfulness? To choose now,
this man, knowing the way vows create their own
lineage. What came of that love
becomes sacred ground
we walk on.

NOTES

The source text for the blackout poems, which function as section breaks in this collection, is the funeral pamphlet biography for Sergeant Bradley Adams. Author unknown.

"Solemnly Spoken": Incorporates language from Psalm 23. Italicized portion from U.S. Military Oath of Enlistment.

"Operation Pegasus Bridge": Quote for Cpl. Sean Stokes originally recounted by journalist, Patrick O' Donnell in *Los Angeles Times* article by John Spano in 2007.

"Oceanside": Italicized portion from the Marines' Hymn.

"Corporal Stokes": Cpl. Sean Stokes was posthumously awarded the Silver Star in 2008. Verified by *Los Angeles Times* article by Tony Perry in 2008.

"The Fox and the Lion" is a reference to the Aseop's fable with the same name.

"Divorce Papers": Epigraph from Congresswoman Barbara Lee from the floor of the U.S. House of Representatives on September 14, 2001, when she was the only Congress member to vote against the Authorization for Use of Military Force after the World Trade Center attacks on September 11, 2001. Italicized text from the Authorization for Use of Military Force.

"Back Azimuth Is This": A back azimuth is a land navigation term meaning to calculate where you currently are based on a known point of where you have been.

"Photosynthesis": After "Fire Diary" by Mark Tredinnick

"The Lion and the Mouse": Italicized text from Émile Durkheim book, *Suicide: A Study in Sociology*. Fable is a perversion of Aesop's story, "The Lion and the Mouse."

ACKNOWLEDGMENTS

Humble thanks to the following publications who have published variations of poems from this collection:

"The Battle of the Eclipse"   *Montreal Poetry Prize Anthology 2020*
"Cliff Diving"   *Porter House Review*
"The Crossing"   *Narrative Magazine*
"Fragmentation," "Enduring Freedom," "Before Leaving" &
    "Deployment"   *Birmingham Poetry Review*
"Liminal"   *Witness Magazine*
"MEDEVAC,"   *War, Literature, and the Arts Journal*
"Oceanside"   *Stone Canoe Journal*
"Walter Reed Hospital"   Heroes' Voices

Special thanks to the following contests in which poems from this collection were selected as finalist, semifinalist, or honorable mention:

Finalist, Montreal International Poetry Prize
Finalist, X.J. Kennedy Poetry Prize
Finalist, Autumn House Press Full-Length Poetry Contest
Finalist, Wheelbarrow Books Poetry Prize
Finalist, *Narrative Magazine*'s 4th Annual Poetry Contest
Finalist, Airlie Prize
Finalist, Tennessee Williams / New Orleans Literary Festival Poetry
Semifinalist, Lexi Rudnitsky First Book Prize in Poetry
2nd Place, *Witness Magazine* Literary Award for Poetry

2nd Place, Porter House Review Editor's Prize in Poetry
3rd Place, Heroes' Voices National Veterans Poetry Contest
Honorable Mention, May Sarton New Hampshire Poetry Prize

I would like to specifically thank my husband, Daniel Levine, who read countless drafts of these poems, gave me constant encouragement when I doubted the necessity of this collection, and took over house projects and childcare to give me the space to complete it. I am forever grateful.

I am indebted to my sister, Sharon Healy, who would not let me get away from the true heart of a poem.

I would like to thank the following individuals who read drafts and provided feedback: Linda Levine, Barry Levine, Rob Gilmor, Jenny Nessel, Evin Moore, Jessica Murray, Adam Vines, Tristan Jih, and my cohort at Lighthouse Writers Poetry Collective.

I also would like to thank Lighthouse Writers Workshop for their Poetry Collective which gave me the space and the guidance to come up with the first draft of this collection under the tutelage of Elizabeth Robinson, and for their Veterans Writing Award (awarded by Steven Dunn) which allowed me to work with Carolyn Forché. I am also grateful to Longleaf Writers Conference for their Baker Veteran Scholarship.

The following teachers have helped me in the making of this collection: Elizabeth Robinson, Bin Ramke, Eleni Sikelianos, and Graham Foust.

Finally, I would like to thank Andrew Saulters and Unicorn Press for having faith in the importance of this project and seeing it through to its final form. Your reading and commentary demonstrated a genuine understanding of what I was trying to achieve in this work.

AMBER ADAMS received her MA in Literary Studies from the University of Denver, and her MA in Counseling from Regis University. Her work has appeared in *Birmingham Poetry Review, Narrative, War Literature and the Arts Journal, Stone Canoe Journal*, and elsewhere. She served in the United States Army Reserves and completed one tour of duty under Operation Iraqi Freedom. She lives in Boulder, CO.

Text in Arno Pro.
Titles in TW Cen.
Cover and text design
by Andrew Saulters.

75 hardbound copies and
400 bound in paper were
produced by Unicorn Press.